10 MINUTE
SATs TESTS
GRAMMAR, PUNCTUATION AND SPELLING

AGES 10–11 YEAR 6

KS2

Scholastic Education, an imprint of Scholastic Ltd

Book End, Range Road, Witney, Oxfordshire, OX29 0YD

Registered office: Westfield Road, Southam, Warwickshire CV47 0RA

www.scholastic.co.uk

British Library Cataloguing-in-Publication Data

A catalogue record for this book is available from the British Library.

ISBN 9781407176079

Printed and bound by Ashford Colour Press

Author
Giles Clare

Editorial
Audrey Stokes, Tracy Kewley, Kate Pedlar, Suzanne Adams

Cover and Series Design
Scholastic Design Team: Nicolle Thomas and Neil Salt

Cover Illustration
Adam Linley @ Beehive Illustration, Visual Generation @ Shutterstock

Contents

How to use this book	4
Grammar and Punctuation Test 1	5
Grammar and Punctuation Test 2	9
Spelling Tests 1 and 2	13
Grammar and Punctuation Test 3	14
Grammar and Punctuation Test 4	18
Spelling Tests 3 and 4	22
Grammar and Punctuation Test 5	23
Grammar and Punctuation Test 6	27
Spelling Tests 5 and 6	31
Grammar and Punctuation Test 7	32
Grammar and Punctuation Test 8	36
Spelling Tests 7 and 8	40
Grammar and Punctuation Test 9	41
Grammar and Punctuation Test 10	45
Spelling Tests 9 and 10	49
Grammar glossary	50
Grammar and Punctuation answers	51
How to administer the spelling tests	59
Spelling test transcripts	60
Progress chart and Reward certificate	63

How to use this book

This book contains ten different Grammar, Punctuation and Spelling tests for Year 6, each containing SATs-style questions. As a whole, the complete set of tests provides broad coverage of the test framework for this age group.

It is intended that children will take around ten minutes to complete each test, although they may work through the spelling tests more quickly. Each test comprises 11 grammar and punctuation questions and four spellings. The ratio of grammar and punctuation questions to spelling questions is similar to that of the National Curriculum tests.

Grammar and punctuation tests

The tests comprise a mixture of question types: some questions require a selected response, where children choose the correct answer from a list; other questions require a constructed response, where children insert a word or punctuation mark, or write a short answer of their own.

Spelling tests

Read each spelling number followed by *The word is...* Read the context sentence and then repeat *The word is...* Leave at least a 12-second gap between spellings. More information can be found on page 59.

The glossary on page 50 provides a useful guide to the ten most important grammatical terms which children need to be familiar with in order to be successful in the Year 6 grammar test.

Test 1
Grammar and Punctuation

10 MINS

Marks

1. Tick the sentences below that contain an **adverb.**

Tick **two**.

That piece of music is really amazing.

There's a fast connection from the airport to the ferry.

My old uncle buys a daily newspaper.

Eventually, the tree rotted away into the soil.

1

2. Underline the **two** words in the passage below that are **antonyms** of each other.

Samir and Ollie had played together since they were small. Unfortunately, their bad behaviour led their parents to decide that it was best to keep them apart.

1

3. Tick **one** box in each row to show whether the underlined words are a **main clause** or a **subordinate clause**.

Marks

Sentence	Main clause	Subordinate clause
Riley and Joe, <u>who were twins from Nottingham</u>, both represented Great Britain at table tennis.		
<u>The old boots</u>, which were covered in mud, <u>were beginning to smell</u>.		
Whenever we go shopping, <u>my baby brother always wants to push the trolley</u>.		
<u>Although the moon was behind the cloud</u>, it was still bright enough to find our way home.		

1

4. Place a **colon** in the correct place in the sentence below.

Amelia has three main hobbies skiing, skydiving and baking.

1

5. Rewrite the sentence below to correct the **nouns** that should have **capital letters**.

Last wednesday, our friend's mum won a trip to the caribbean.

_____

_____

1

KEEP IT GOING!

Marks

6. Draw a line to match each word to the correct **prefix** to make an **adjective** with the opposite meaning.

dis

un

ir

likely

responsible

advantage

1

7. Tick **two** boxes to show where the missing **inverted commas** should go.

Freddie explained, I'm sorry I'm late. The bus broke down.

1

8. Underline **all** of the **determiners** in the sentence below.

The young chef chopped twenty carrots with his sharp knife.

1

9. Rearrange the words in the **statement** below to make it a **question**. You will need to add or change words. Remember to **punctuate** your sentence correctly.

Statement: She always spends so long in the shower.

1

10. Replace the underlined word or words in each sentence with the correct **possessive pronoun**.

Those old toys belong to <u>your sister</u>. They are _____.

<u>Our dog</u> is scared of the storm. It's hiding in _____ bed.

The garden is owned by <u>us</u>. It belongs to _____ family.

Marks

1

11. a. Underline the **two modal verbs** in the sentence below.

My parcel may arrive tomorrow, although I might not be at home.

1

b. Explain the job of the modal verbs in this sentence.

_____

_____

1

Well done! END OF GRAMMAR & PUNCTUATION TEST 1!

Test 2
Grammar and Punctuation

Marks

I. Tick the sentence that must end with a **question mark**.

Tick **one.**

How this place has changed since last year

What a spectacular fireworks display that was

How far is it to the next village

It's an important question to ask

1

2. Replace the underlined words in the sentence with their **contracted forms**.

You <u>should not</u> tell lies. <u>It is</u> naughty. <u>I will</u> be cross.

↑　　　　↑　　　　↑

1

3. Circle the **two noun phrases** in the sentence.

The worst thing about Adam is his smelly feet, which really stink!

1

4. Circle **one** word in each pair to complete the sentences using **Standard English**.

We couldn't see **nothing / anything**.

You should **have / of** left for school already.

1

Marks

5. Tick **one** box in each row to show whether the sentence is written in the **active voice** or the **passive voice**.

Sentence	Active	Passive
My dog loves sticks and tennis balls.		
Actually, bread is quite simple to make.		
The spy was arrested by the police.		

1

6. Complete the passage with **adjectives** derived from the verbs in brackets. One has been done for you.

The lesson after lunch was really <u>boring</u> [bore].

The grandmaster made a _____ [decide] move to win the chess match.

Maddie's performance was greeted with _____ [enthuse] applause.

1

7. Circle the **two co-ordinating conjunctions** in the sentences below.

Virat was often late but his friend Ravi was always on time. Whilst Ravi waited for Virat, he would read a book or whistle a tune.

1

Marks

8. Which **punctuation mark** should be used in the place indicated by the arrow?

Alistair, 23, a student who was always asking questions lost his laptop on the bus.

Tick **one**.

a question mark ☐

a full stop ☐

a bracket ☐

a comma ☐

1

9. Complete the sentences below, using the **past progressive tense** of the verbs in the boxes.

We _____ really fast until the train broke down.

travel

bake

get

Whilst mum _____, I _____ hungrier by the minute.

KEEP IT GOING!

1

Marks

10. Complete the sentence below by writing the **prepositions** from the box in the correct places. Use each preposition only once.

> until
>
> after
>
> for

We are not leaving _____ Paris _____ Saturday,

just _____ lunch.

1

---

11. Explain how the different **prefixes** mean that the two sentences below have different meanings.

a. The football manager gave a <u>prematch</u> interview.

This means that the manager was talking _____

_____

1

b. The football manager gave a <u>postmatch</u> interview.

This means that the manager was talking _____

_____

1

Well done! END OF GRAMMAR & PUNCTUATION TEST 2!

Spelling test 1

Marks

1. Ollie was Joshua's new best _____.

2. Evie _____ it was probably time to go home.

3. You can use a _____ to look up word meanings.

4. Riley enjoyed _____ and biology at school.

4

Well done! END OF SPELLING TEST 1!

Spelling test 2

Marks

1. The washing _____ was making a strange noise.

2. The _____ soared in the desert.

3. My Uncle Stan always _____ to drink cold tea.

4. Rohan took his broken _____ to the recycling centre.

4

Well done! END OF SPELLING TEST 2!

Marks

1. Circle the **two** words in the sentences below that contain an **apostrophe** for **possession**.

"It's going to be dark soon," said Jack's brother worriedly. "We should've stayed at the hikers' shelter."

1

2. Label the boxes with **V** (verb), **S** (subject) and **O** (object) to show the parts of the sentence.

The lion ate the antelope.

↑   ↑   ↑
☐   ☐   ☐

1

3. Tick **one** box in each row to show whether the **commas** are used correctly in the sentence.

Sentence	Commas used correctly	Commas used incorrectly
My favourite sports are hockey, basketball, tennis and snowboarding.		
The planet Jupiter, which is mostly made of gas and liquid spins on its axis, every 10 hours.		
The useless builder shouted, screamed, groaned, and, finally threw down his tools.		
Whenever I feel upset and lonely, I ring my grandad, who cheers me up with silly jokes.		

1

Marks

4. What is the function of the sentence below?

Before the tsunami arrives, leave town as quickly as possible.

Tick **one**.

a statement ☐

a question ☐

a command ☐

an exclamation ☐

1

5. Circle the word in the sentence below that is in the **wrong tense**.

You must go to the chemist, bought some pills and take them immediately.

1

6. Which sentence is written in **Standard English**?

Tick **one**.

I don't want those shoes because I want them ones. ☐

Me and Rhys are doing a run for charity. ☐

Ain't it gonna snow later? ☐

We really should've won the tournament today. ☐

1

KEEP IT GOING!

15

7. Draw a line to match each **verb** to the correct **suffix** to make a **noun**.

Verb	Suffix
impress	ence
develop	ion
refer	ment

Marks

1

8. Complete the sentence below so that it uses the **subjunctive form**.

The prime minister insisted that the votes _____ counted again.

1

9. Replace the underlined word or words in each sentence with the correct **pronoun**.

If William works hard, <u>William</u> might be given a pay rise.

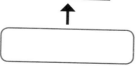

There were some ponies in the field but our dog chased <u>the ponies</u>.

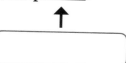

1

10 MINS

Marks

10. You are helping a friend to correct the punctuation in the box below. Which **two** pieces of advice should you give her?

The angry gardener exclaimed "Youre standing on my flowers!"

Tick **two**.

The sentence should end with a full stop after the inverted commas. ☐

There should be an apostrophe between the 'you' and 're' of 'youre'. ☐

There should be a comma after 'exclaimed'. ☐

There should be an exclamation mark after 'exclaimed'. ☐

There should be a comma after 'gardener'. ☐

1

11. Complete these sentences by adding the correct **relative pronoun** to each **relative clause.**

Anika's sister, _____ was tall and thin, became a famous high jumper.

The houses _____ are due to be demolished were flooded last night.

Her phone, _____ was completely covered in paint, didn't work anymore.

The policeman, _____ job it was to protect the president, spotted the assassin.

2

Well done! END OF GRAMMAR & PUNCTUATION TEST 3!

Test 4
Grammar and Punctuation

10 MINS

Marks

1. Underline the **main clause** in each sentence below.

However early Micah went to bed on Sunday evenings, he always felt tired on Mondays.

Olivia left for school, even though it was a bit early.

If I were you, I would leave immediately.

1

2. Draw a line to match each sentence to its **function**. Use each function only **once**.

Sentence	Function
What a silly mistake I made	command
You have finished your homework, haven't you	statement
Make sure you remember your PE kit today	exclamation
I understand that you are feeling nervous	question

1

3. Which sentence uses the **hyphen** correctly?

Tick one.

The strange looking-old woman was his sister in-law. ☐

The strange-looking old woman was his sister-in-law. ☐

The strange-looking-old woman was his sister-in-law. ☐

The strange looking old-woman was his sister-in-law. ☐

1

18

Marks

4. Tick **one** box in each row to show whether each underlined word is used as a **noun** or **verb**.

Sentence	Used as a noun	Used as a verb
The package was delivered to the wrong <u>address</u> again.		
The correct way to <u>address</u> the Queen is "Your Majesty".		
My dad <u>coaches</u> the Under 11 cricket team.		
The children travelled on two <u>coaches</u> to the theme park.		

1

5. What does the **root** <u>mari</u> mean in the word family below?

sub**mar**ine   **mari**time   aqua**mar**ine   **mari**ner

Tick **one**.

under ☐

water ☐

liquid ☐

sea ☐

1

10 MINS

Marks

6. Underline the **verb form** that is in the **past perfect** in the sentence below.

My dad complained, "How many times have I told you? If you had listened to me, you wouldn't have lost your phone."

1

7. Rewrite the following sentence to place the **adverbial phrase** at the beginning. Make sure you punctuate your sentence correctly.

Self-driving vehicles will be a common sight a few years from now.

_____

_____

1

8. Insert a **semi-colon** in the correct place in the sentence below:

A flash of lightning lit up the garden a second later, thunder rattled the windows in their frames.

1

9. Tick **one** box in each row to show if each sentence uses **formal** or **informal vocabulary**.

Sentence	Formal	Informal
There are loads of things wrong with my new car.		
There are a number of issues with my new vehicle.		
I request that you rectify the problems at your earliest convenience.		
I want you to fix the problems as soon as you can.		

1

Marks

10. Complete the sentences below, using the **simple past tense** of the verbs in the boxes.

My neighbours just _____ a young girl.

⬆

| adopt |

At the beach, we _____ and then _____ under the palm trees.

⬆   ⬆

| swim | | sleep |

1

11. a. Circle the words in this passage where the **apostrophe** is **not** needed.

Six month's ago, Henry's grandad completed his round-the-world trip. He travelled all the way on two wheel's after borrowing his neighbour's bike!

b. Explain why the words you have circled do not need an apostrophe.

_____

_____

1

Well done! END OF GRAMMAR & PUNCTUATION TEST 4!

Spelling tests 3 & 4

Spelling test 3

1. Water from the bath was dripping through the _____.

2. The town was invaded by a _____ of rats.

3. Denise _____ most of the answers in the test.

4. The pirate captain dropped the _____ map overboard.

4

Well done! END OF SPELLING TEST 3!

Spelling test 4

Marks

1. The boxer entered the _____ competition.

2. The shipwreck was _____ beneath the waves.

3. Flora decided she wanted to become a _____.

4. Spicy food can cause a burning _____ in your mouth.

4

Well done! END OF SPELLING TEST 4!

Test 5
Grammar and Punctuation

10 MINS

Marks

1. Underline the **conjunctions** in the sentence below.

Priya hated fried food until she tried battered fish when she was on holiday.

1

2. Tick all of the sentences that should end with a **question mark**.

You promised to help me, didn't you ☐

How was the movie ☐

What an enormous meal that was ☐

Should I go and fill the car up ☐

1

3. Rewrite the following sentence to put the **subordinate clause** first. Remember to punctuate your sentence correctly.

We are going to miss our flight to Paris unless the taxi arrives soon.

_____

_____

_____

1

4. Tick all the **synonyms** for 'sluggish'.

drowsy ☐

slimy ☐

slow ☐

weary ☐

1

23

Marks

5. Change the underlined words to **plurals**.

The <u>chef</u> kept the <u>knife</u> in the special <u>box</u>.

↑   ↑   ↑

☐   ☐   ☐

1

6. Tick **one** box to show the correct place to insert a **single dash** in the sentence below.

There was a figure in the shadows or – was it just my imagination? ☐

There was a figure – in the shadows or was it just my imagination? ☐

There was a figure in the shadows or was it – just my imagination? ☐

There was a figure in the shadows – or was it just my imagination? ☐

1

7. Summer camp activities include: learning life-saving skills in the pool; building a shelter in the woods; or climbing down the cliffs by the sea.

On the lines below, write a list of the activities described above using **bullet points**. Remember to punctuate your answer correctly.

At summer camp, you can choose from:

_____

_____

_____

1

10 MINS

Marks

8. Fill in the gaps below using the **present progressive tense** of the verbs in the box.

decide
↓

Whilst we _____ what to do,

time _____ out.

↑
run

1

9. What are the underlined words in the sentence below?

You'll find a magical world <u>beneath the sea</u> just waiting to be discovered.

Tick **one.**

a main clause ☐

a prepositional phrase ☐

a subordinate clause ☐

an adverbial phrase ☐

1

10. Tick **two** boxes to show where the missing **pair of brackets** should go.

☐   ☐   ☐ ☐
↓   ↓   ↓ ↓

The concert was delayed by ten minutes again the violinist was always late .
↑
☐

1

10 MINS

11. Look at this passage.

Marks

> Soon, I am going on a special holiday. We will travel to the beautiful island of Bali by air. Unfortunately, the plane leaves at six in the morning. It will be amazing though: we are going to stay in a hotel on the tropical beach.

a. Tick **all** the statements that describe this passage.

It contains three adjectives. ☐

It is all written in the future tense. ☐

It uses a colon to introduce a list. ☐

It contains two adverbs. ☐

1

b. List all the **adjectives** from the passage on the line below.

_____

1

Well done! END OF GRAMMAR & PUNCTUATION TEST 5!

Marks

1. Tick the sentence that uses **capital letters** and **full stops** correctly.

Tick **one.**

Diwali is a Special time of year for hindus. It is a festival of lights. ☐

Diwali is a special time of year for Hindus it is a festival of lights. ☐

Diwali is a special time of year for hindus. It is a Festival of Lights ☐

Diwali is a special time of year for Hindus. It is a festival of lights. ☐

1

2. Rearrange the words in the question below to make it a **statement**. Use only the given words. Remember to punctuate your sentence correctly.

Question: Were you always interested in animals?

Statement: _____

1

3. Tick **one** box in each row to show how the **modal verb** affects the meaning of the sentence.

Sentence	Modal verb indicates how possible it is	Modal verb indicates how necessary it is
We must decorate the sitting room soon.		
My dad will be really cross.		
I ought to go home now.		
They may go to Japan next year.		

1

4. Replace the **subject** in this sentence with a different one. Write your answer on the line below.

The criminal was caught in a trap.

Marks

1

5. Underline the word in each row that does not belong to the same **word family**.

a. signal   signpost   sightless   insignificant

b. recovery   coves   discover   coverage

c. presentation   depressing impressive   expressed

1

6. Rewrite this sentence so that it is in the **past tense**.

When Molly goes swimming, her brother Ashton teaches her how to dive.

1

7. Explain how the **apostrophe** changes the meaning in these sentences.

Harmony always wanted to hang out with her sister's friends.

Harmony always wanted to hang out with her sisters' friends.

1

10 MINS

Marks

8. Join each sentence to the correct label.

Alex didn't do anything wrong.

Me and Alex are going to watch television.

Harry invited Alex and me to tea.

I ain't been to Harry's house before.

Standard English

non-Standard English

◯

1

9. What are the words <u>the best day of the week</u> in the sentence below?

I reckon Sunday is definitely <u>the best day of the week</u>.

Tick **one**.

a subordinate clause ☐

a noun phrase ☐

a fronted adverbial ☐

a prepositional phrase ☐

◯

1

10. Some of the **punctuation** is missing in the text below. Insert the correct punctuation into each of the boxes.

☐ Watch out ☐☐ shouted Mum ☐☐ The oven is very hot ☐☐

◯

1

11. Read this sentence:

My great aunt and uncle were very demanding: you had to do everything _____ way.

Marks

a. Choose the best **pronoun** to fit in the space in the sentence.

Tick **one**.

my ☐

his ☐

their ☐

her ☐

1

b. The word <u>very</u> is used as:

Tick **one**.

an adjective ☐

a conjunction ☐

a determiner ☐

an adverb ☐

1

Well done! END OF GRAMMAR & PUNCTUATION TEST 6!

Spelling tests 5 & 6

 **10 MINS**

Spelling test 5

1. The great lion let out a _____ roar.

2. Children should be careful when using _____ networks.

3. The school fair was a _____ success.

4. My favourite sweets are no longer _____ in the shops.

4

Well done! END OF SPELLING TEST 5!

Spelling test 6

1. My mum is looking for a job _____ near home.

2. The _____ practised his tricks for hour after hour.

3. A tiny mouse crept out _____ from behind the fridge.

4. Samit was very interested in _____ matters.

4

Well done! END OF SPELLING TEST 6!

Test 7
Grammar and Punctuation

10 MINS

Marks

1. Which of these sentences is a **command**?

Tick **one**.

At six o'clock, you should do your guitar practice. ☐

When you hear the starting pistol, run as fast as you can. ☐

I am ordering you to follow my instructions. ☐

We want you to pick up all the litter you dropped. ☐

1

2. Insert **commas** in the correct places in the sentence below.

Fish and chips pizzas sausages and kebabs often contain large amounts of fat.

1

3. Circle the **subordinating conjunction** in each sentence below.

As soon as the rain stopped, the sun burst through the clouds.

Connor will win the prize provided he arrives on time.

1

4. Rewrite this sentence making sure the **tense** is consistent.

The two brothers had left school, start a business and became very successful.

_____

_____

1

10 MINS

Marks

5. This sentence has a **main clause**, a **subordinate clause** and an **adverbial** in it.

After football in the rain, Henry washed his knees, which were covered in mud.

Tick the **subordinate clause.**   Tick the **adverbial.**

Tick **one.**   Tick **one.**

After football in the rain ☐	After football in the rain ☐
Henry washed his knees ☐	Henry washed his knees ☐
which were covered in mud ☐	which were covered in mud ☐

1

6. Draw lines to join each word to the correct **contraction.**

could have

could'of

could've

it is

it's

its'

shall not

shan't

shalln't

1

Marks

7. Draw a line to match each **determiner** to the correct **question**. Use each determiner only **once**.

Determiner   **Question**

an

that

most

Why is _____ person staring?

Is that _____ invitation?

When are _____ visitors expected?

1

8. Tick all the sentences that contain a **preposition**.

The weary traveller walked along the cliff path. ☐

After school, Lenny went to boxing. ☐

Before we leave, I am going to phone Grandma. ☐

You must not speak until the test is finished. ☐

1

9. Rewrite the sentence below so that is in the **active voice**. Remember to punctuate your sentence correctly.

The fishing boats were destroyed by the powerful storm.

_____

_____

1

Marks

10. Explain how the use of **commas** makes the meaning of these two sentences different.

The passengers, who were hot and bored, complained to the bus driver.

The passengers who were hot and bored complained to the bus driver.

_____

_____

_____

1

11. a. Complete the table below by adding a **suffix** to each noun to make an **adjective**.

Noun	Adjective
adventure	
artist	
fortune	

1

b. Add a **prefix** to one of the **adjectives** to make a word with the opposite meaning. Write this **antonym** below.

_____

1

Well done! END OF GRAMMAR & PUNCTUATION TEST 7!

Test 8
Grammar and Punctuation

10 MINS

Marks

1. Underline the **verbs** in this sentence.

When I was young, I lived on a tiny island off the coast of Africa.

1

2. Tick the sentence that must end with an **exclamation mark**.

Tick **one**.

What time was it when you got home ☐

How irritating that salesman was ☐

How long is that piece of liquorice ☐

What kind of food do you serve here ☐

1

3. Insert two **semi-colons** in the correct places in the sentence below.

These are the places I would like to go one day: Paris in the spring sunshine the snow-capped mountains of Switzerland and Cairo with its amazing pyramids.

1

4. Which of the events below is **least likely** to happen?

Tick **one**.

They may come for tea this evening. ☐

They must come for tea this evening. ☐

They will come for tea this evening. ☐

They shall come for tea this evening. ☐

1

Marks

5. Tick one box to show where the missing **colon** should go.

☐   ☐
↓   ↓

We were really disappointed the food was cold, the table was dirty and the waiter was rude.

↑   ↑
☐   ☐

1

6. Underline the **relative clause** in the sentence below.

The piano tuner, a tiny man from Dundee with an explosion of grey curly hair, hummed a pretty tune as he walked home.

1

7. Add these **suffixes** to the nouns below to make **verbs**. You will need to use one suffix more than once. Rewrite the words in full. You may need to add or take away letters.

ise   ate   ify

pollen   _____

apology   _____

class   _____

television _____

1

Marks

8. Rewrite this sentence in **Standard English**.

He were wearing them shoes what he bought last week.

_____

_____

1

9. Underline the **pronouns** in these sentences.

We told them about the power cut but they went to his house anyway.

My rabbit, which loves carrots, likes sleeping on our sofa.

1

10. Insert a **hyphen** into the sentence below to make the meaning clearer.

There was a hand made yellow skirt in the window display.

1

Marks

11. a. The verbs in this sentence are all in different forms of the past tense. Draw a line from each sentence to the correct **tense** of each verb.

| The boys were playing catch in the garden. |

simple past

| The boys have played catch in the garden. |

past progressive

| The boys played catch in the garden. |

past perfect

| The boys had played catch in the garden. |

present perfect

1

b. Rewrite the sentence about boys playing catch in the garden in the **present progressive** tense.

_____

_____

1

Well done! END OF GRAMMAR & PUNCTUATION TEST 8!

Spelling test 7

Marks

1. Mia used watercolours to paint the beautiful _____.

2. The swimmer was _____ waving for help.

3. General Fox ordered the _____ to begin the next day.

4. The sports car accelerated and _____ the slow lorry.

4

Well done! END OF SPELLING TEST 7!

Spelling test 8

Marks

1. The human body uses _____ to build and repair muscles.

2. You should wash a burn _____ under cold running water.

3. Tijan dreamed about becoming a _____ footballer.

4. We didn't have _____ petrol for the journey.

4

Well done! END OF SPELLING TEST 8!

Marks

1. Circle the **co-ordinating conjunctions** in the sentences.

Although it was sunny, Bertie stayed indoors and played computer games.

If you ask me, you should go to the doctor or go home but go to bed.

1

2. Underline the **nouns** in the sentence.

The little boy was nervous about starting at his new school.

Underline the **subject** of the sentence.

This pizza was ordered by you, wasn't it?

1

3. Add a **prefix** to each of these adjectives to give them a different, but not opposite, meaning.

_____take   _____tired   _____angular

1

4. Insert **two commas** in the correct places in the sentence below.

Last Sunday evening we watched an amazing nature documentary whilst my nan fell asleep on the sofa and snored loudly.

1

5. Draw a line to match the correct **question tag** to the each sentence to complete them.

Marks

The girls forgot to buy the chocolates,

aren't we?

Remember to do your homework,

shouldn't I?

I guess I should try harder.

won't you?

After school, we're going swimming,

didn't they?

1

6. Which option completes the sentence below so that it uses the **subjunctive mood**?

If I _____ to describe Rosalie, I would say she was clever and kind.

Tick **one**.

was ☐

be ☐

were ☐

are ☐

1

7. Rewrite this sentence by changing the verbs from the **simple past tense** to the **simple present**.

Gethin often went walking in the mountains but he usually forgot his coat.

_____

_____

1

Marks

8. Rewrite the sentence below as **direct speech**. Remember to punctuate your sentence correctly.

Fatima asked Zara if she wanted to come to a party that evening.

Fatima asked Zara,

_____

_____

_____

1

9. Write one more word for each **word family**.

doubt   doubtful   _____

pure   impure   _____

day   midday   _____

1

10. Tick **one** box in each row to show the correct type of each underlined **adverb**.

Marks

Sentence	Adverb indicating when	Adverb indicating where	Adverb indicating how
Mum's phone rang <u>noisily</u> inside her bag.			
She would <u>eventually</u> realise that Tyler had been lying.			
When the storm started, our dog quickly ran <u>indoors</u>.			

1

11. a. Underline the two **noun phrases** in the sentence below.

According to my uncle Joseph, this coming winter is going to be very cold.

Underline the **clause** in the sentence below.

According to my uncle Joseph, this coming winter is going to be very cold.

1

b. What **class of word** is in a clause but not in a phrase?

_____

1

Well done! END OF GRAMMAR & PUNCTUATION TEST 9!

Marks

1. Insert **full stops** in the correct places in the passage below.

My mum is always worrying about losing her purse I look after my pocket money in a jar, which I keep next to my bed so that no-one can steal it How do you look after your money?

1

2. Join and rewrite these sentences using a different **conjunction** in each sentence.

| so | because | after |

We should get off the beach. The tide is about to turn.

_____

_____

I must tidy up the house. Our visitors have left.

_____

_____

1

3. Underline the **two subordinate clauses** in this sentence.

Last week, my friend Jamie, who was born in Sheffield, fell into a pond while he was eating an ice-cream.

1

4. In the sentence below, Lucas lost his keys before his neighbours invited him.

Complete the sentence with the correct **verb form**.

Because Lucas _____ lost his keys, his neighbours invited him to stay for the night.

1

5. Tick **one** box in each row to identify the underlined words in each sentence.

Sentence	Phrase	Clause	Conjunction
<u>As soon as</u> the dog barked, the thief ran away.			
<u>Oscar really likes the colour green.</u>			
Erin picked <u>some ripe, red apples</u> in the orchard.			

1

6. Draw lines to the correct labels for each sentence in this conversation.

What a fool I've been!		statement
What did you do?		exclamation
I left my passport at home.		command
Go and fetch it quickly!		question

1

Marks

7. Circle the **prepositions** in the sentences below.

Today I am going swimming before breakfast.

There is a delay due to some faulty traffic lights.

The elephant calf trotted behind its mother.

1

8. Look at the **apostrophes for possession** in the underlined nouns. Draw lines to the correct labels for each noun.

| on the <u>dog's</u> fur |

| in <u>Angus's</u> bag |

singular
noun

| under the <u>children's</u> clothes. |

plural
noun

| through the <u>neighbours'</u> letterbox |

1

9. Choose the **suffix** that will change all of these words into **nouns**. Use the same suffix for all four words. Rewrite the new words in full in the space provided. You may need to change some letters.

ly   ance   ment

important   _____

instant   _____

resist   _____

appear   _____

1

Marks

10. Rewrite the sentence below to include a **relative clause** between the commas.

The strange bird, _____ ,
flapped its wings and flew away.

_____

_____

_____

1

11. a. Each of the sentences below is missing **one** piece of **punctuation**. Insert the missing punctuation in the correct place.

The tall wizard, who lived in a tower full of cobwebs cast a spell on the village.

His parcel finally arrived it was already two months late).

When he found his spelling mistakes – there were over 100 of them the author shook his head in horror.

1

b. In each sentence above, the completed punctuation is used to insert:

Tick one.

a subordinate clause ☐

an adverbial phrase ☐

a parenthesis ☐

a relative clause ☐

1

Well done! END OF GRAMMAR & PUNCTUATION TEST 10!

Spelling test 9

1. The instructions for building the furniture were _____.

2. The bullet travelled straight _____ the brick.

3. Otto was put in the group for _____.

4. _____ , the injured climber managed to survive.

4

Well done! END OF SPELLING TEST 9!

Spelling test 10

1. The sprinter was always trying to improve his _____.

2. Storms can cause _____ with TV and radio broadcasts.

3. Luke couldn't _____ that he had lost the game.

4. My grandma left suddenly without _____.

4

Well done! END OF SPELLING TEST 10!

Grammar glossary
The 'Top ten trickiest terms' you should know

1. Noun phrase
A <u>noun phrase</u> is a group of words that adds more information about a noun. The **noun** is the most important word in the phrase.

*<u>Some huge, ugly, brown</u> **insects** crawled over <u>the pile of rotting</u> **vegetables**.*

2. Determiner
A **determiner** comes at the start of a noun phrase and makes it more general (eg some) or specific (eg the).

***Some** huge, ugly, brown insects crawled over **the** pile of rotting vegetables.*

3. Fronted adverbial
An <u>adverbial</u> is a phrase that describes when, how or where something is taking place. A **fronted adverbial** comes at the front of the sentence and is separated by a comma from the main clause.

*<u>**At nine o'clock every evening**</u>, Tom stood <u>on his head</u> <u>in his bedroom</u>.*

4. Perfect tense
The perfect tense is used to describe something that took place in the past. The <u>present perfect</u> describes something that began in the past but may still continue into the present. The **past perfect** describes something that occurred before another action in the past.

I <u>have worked</u> at the hospital for two years.

*She **had fallen** asleep before the film started.*

5. Exclamation
There are four sentence types: statements, questions, commands and exclamations. Although statements and commands can end in an exclamation mark, in the test, only statements that start with 'What' or 'How' and end with exclamation marks are accepted as exclamations.

What a strange day it has been!

How clever that old man is!

6. Modal verb
A <u>modal verb</u> goes before another verb to show how possible, certain or necessary something is.

The weather <u>may</u> turn colder next week.

Grandad <u>should</u> arrive home before Thursday.

You <u>must</u> finish your peas before you have a pudding.

7. Subordinating conjunction
A **subordinating conjunction** is a linking word or phrase. It links a <u>subordinate clause</u> to a main clause. The subordinate clause can come at the start, the middle or the end of a sentence.

*<u>**After**</u> <u>I had packed my bag</u>, I put on my coat.*

*The white dog, **which** <u>had a long fluffy tail</u>, chased the lorry*

*She loved Scotland **even though** <u>she had never been there</u>.*

8. Parenthesis
A <u>parenthesis</u> is additional information inserted into a sentence. It is separated from the rest of the sentence by a pair of commas, brackets or dashes. You can remove a parenthesis and the sentence will still make sense.

Mr Smith<u>, a bald poet from Derby,</u> wrote his books in a shed.

Last week, my aunt won a big prize in the lottery <u>(over £1000)</u>.

Suddenly, I saw Jimmy <u>– that thin Jimmy with long hair –</u> jump out from behind a rock.

9. Clause
A clause is a group of words that contains at least a **subject** and a <u>verb</u>. There are three types: main clauses, subordinate clauses and relative clauses. Clauses can be linked by co-ordinating or subordinating conjunctions or by relative pronouns. Only a main clause makes sense as a sentence on its own.

He <u>jumps</u>.

*I <u>was singing</u> while **she** <u>was playing</u> the guitar.*

The new computer, which <u>used</u> the latest software, <u>stopped working</u>.

10. Synonyms and antonyms
A **synonym** is a word with the same meaning as another word. An <u>antonym</u> is a word with the opposite meaning of another word.

*Happy: **cheerful**, **glad**, **merry**, **pleased***

Happy: <u>sad</u>, <u>unhappy</u>, <u>upset</u>, <u>miserable</u>

Answers
Grammar and Punctuation

Q	Mark scheme for Grammar and Punctuation Test 1	Marks
1	**Award 1 mark** for **two** correct sentences ticked: That piece of music is really amazing. Eventually, the tree rotted away into the soil. **Grammar essentials:** Adverbs often tell you more about a verb. However, in this case, the adverb 'really' is used to describe the adjective 'amazing'; the adverb 'eventually' is used to describe the whole clause after the comma.	1
2	**Award 1 mark** if 'together' and 'apart' are underlined. **Grammar essentials:** Antonyms are words that are opposite in meaning. Synonyms are words with the same meaning.	1
3	**Award 1 mark** if all are correct: subordinate clause, main clause, main clause, subordinate clause. **Grammar essentials:** A main clause must make sense on its own. A subordinate clause always starts with a conjunction or a relative pronoun.	1
4	**Award 1 mark** for a correctly placed colon: Amelia has three main hobbies: skiing, skydiving and baking. **Punctuation essentials:** A colon can be used to introduce a list.	1
5	**Award 1 mark** if 'Wednesday' and 'Caribbean' are capitalised. **Grammar essentials:** Days of the week and place names need to begin with a capital letter.	1
6	**Award 1 mark** if all are correct: unlikely, irresponsible, disadvantage. **Punctuation essentials:** A prefix is added to the front of a word to alter the meaning, often to its opposite.	1
7	**Award 1 mark** for correct positioning of inverted commas: Freddie explained, **"**I'm sorry I'm late. The bus broke down.**"** **Punctuation essentials:** Inverted commas are also called speech marks. They should mark the start and end of the exact words being spoken.	1
8	**Award 1 mark** for **three** determiners underlined: <u>The</u> young chef chopped <u>twenty</u> carrots with <u>his</u> sharp knife. **Grammar essentials:** A determiner is used at the start of a noun phrase to make it more specific, or to show quantity or possession.	1
9	**Award 1 mark** if the question makes sense and a question mark has been added. For example: Does she always spend so long in the shower? **Grammar /punctuation essentials:** Questions often start with 'does' (or 'do') and they must end with a question mark.	1
10	**Award 1 mark** for all **three** correct: They are <u>hers</u>. It's hiding in <u>its</u> bed. It belongs to <u>our</u> family. **Grammar essentials:** Possessive pronouns show who or what a noun belongs to. They can be used with nouns (its, our) and to replace them (hers).	1
11	**a. Award 1 mark** if 'may' and 'might' are underlined. **b. Award 1 mark** for the following, or similar: The modal verbs show how possible it is. **Grammar essentials:** Modal verbs are found in front of other verbs. They express degrees of possibility, certainty or necessity.	2
	Total	12

Q	Mark scheme for Grammar and Punctuation Test 2	Marks
1	**Award 1 mark** if the correct sentence is ticked: How far is it to the next village? **Grammar essentials:** Exclamations can start with question words ('how' or 'what') but they are not posing a question.	1
2	**Award 1 mark** if all are correct: shouldn't, It's, I'll **Punctuation essentials:** A contraction is when two words are joined. The apostrophe shows exactly where letters have been removed. 'It's' always means 'it is'.	1
3	**Award 1 mark** if both are correct: The worst thing about Adam; his smelly feet. **Grammar essentials:** A noun phrase is a group of words that give more detail about the noun. (Here the nouns are 'Adam' and 'feet'.)	1
4	**Award 1 mark** if both are correct: anything, have. **Grammar essentials:** 'We couldn't see nothing' would be a double negative, which is non-Standard English (grammatically incorrect). The use of 'of' instead of 'have' in constructions such as 'should have' and 'could have' is a common error caused by people writing what they hear.	1
5	**Award 1 mark** if all are correct: active, active, passive. **Grammar essentials:** A passive sentence often includes the word 'by'.	1
6	**Award 1 mark** if both are correct: decisive, enthusiastic. **Grammar essentials:** Adjectives describe nouns and can be created from verbs by adding different suffixes and prefixes.	1
7	**Award 1 mark** if both are correct: but, or. **Grammar essentials:** Co-ordinating conjunctions join words or clauses of equal importance. 'Whilst' is a subordinating conjunction that introduces a subordinate clause.	1
8	**Award 1 mark** if 'a comma' is ticked. **Punctuation essentials:** A comma is required to mark the end of the relative clause introduced by the relative pronoun 'who'.	1
9	**Award 1 mark** if all are correct: were travelling, was baking, was getting. **Grammar essentials:** The past progressive tense describes ongoing events in the past.	1
10	**Award 1 mark** if all are correct: for, until, after. **Grammar essentials:** Prepositions come before nouns to show where or when something is happening. They also indicate destination or direction of travel (for Paris).	1
11	**a. Award 1 mark** for a correct explanation: This means that the manager was talking <u>before the match took place</u>. **b. Award 1 mark** for a correct explanation: This means that the manager was talking <u>after the match took place</u>. **Grammar essentials:** Prefixes change the meaning of the root word (match), often to give words their opposite meanings.	2

| | | **Total** | **12** |

Q	Mark scheme for Grammar and Punctuation Test 3	Marks
1	**Award 1 mark** if both are correct: Jack's, hikers'. **Punctuation essentials:** Apostrophes show either possession or a contraction. Here, the brother belongs to Jack (therefore 'Jack's') and the shelter belongs to more than one hiker (therefore 'hikers'').	1
2	**Award 1 mark** if all are correct: 'The lion' (S) 'ate' (V) 'the antelope' (O). **Grammar essentials:** The usual word order in English is subject, verb, object.	1
3	**Award 1 mark** if all are correct: correctly, incorrectly, incorrectly, correctly. **Punctuation essentials:** Commas can be used to separate items in lists (but not before 'and') or separate subordinate clauses.	1
4	**Award 1 mark** if 'a command' is ticked. **Grammar essentials:** The verb 'leave' is in the imperative form (second person) at the start of the main clause.	1
5	**Award 1 mark** if 'bought' is circled. **Grammar essentials:** The verbs 'go' and 'take' are in the present tense. 'Bought' is the odd-one-out as it is in the past tense. The correct form of the verb is 'buy'.	1

6 **Award 1 mark** if 'We really should've won the tournament today' is ticked.
Grammar /punctuation essentials: Contractions such as 'should've' are allowed in Standard English, but not in formal language.

1

7 **Award 1 mark** if all are correct: impression, development, reference.
Grammar essentials: Suffixes are added to the end of root words.

1

8 **Award 1 mark** for: be (The prime minister insisted that the votes **be** counted again.)
Grammar essentials: Here, the subjunctive verb form is used to express something that should happen.

1

9 **Award 1 mark** if both are correct: he, them.
Grammar essentials: A pronoun replaces a noun or noun phrase to avoid repetition.

1

10 **Award 1 mark** if both are correct.
There should be an apostrophe between the 'you' and 're' of 'youre'.
There should be a comma after 'exclaimed'.
Grammar /punctuation essentials: 'You're' is a contraction of 'you are' (the apostrophe indicates where the 'a' has been removed). A comma is required to separate the narrative part of the sentence from the direct speech.

1

11 **Award 2 marks** if all are correct; award 1 mark if 3 are correct: who, that, which, whose.
Grammar essentials: A relative pronoun introduces a type of subordinate clause called a relative clause, which refers back to a noun or noun phrase.

2

Total **12**

Q	Mark scheme for Grammar and Punctuation Test 4	Marks

1 **Award 1 mark** if all are correct.
However early Micah went to bed on Sunday evenings, <u>he always felt tired on Mondays</u>.
<u>Olivia left for school</u>, even though it was a bit early.
If I were you, <u>I would leave immediately</u>.
Grammar essentials: A main clause contains at least a subject and a verb and makes sense on its own.

1

2 **Award 1 mark** if all are correct.
What a silly mistake I made – exclamation
You have finished your homework, haven't you – question
Make sure you remember your PE kit today – command
I understand that you are feeling nervous – statement.
Grammar essentials: There are four different sentence functions. Exclamations start with 'how' or 'what' (and end with an exclamation mark, but the punctuation is omitted here for the purpose of the test).

1

3 **Award 1 mark** for: The strange-looking old woman was his sister-in-law.
Punctuation essentials: Here, the hyphens are used to make compound words.

1

4 **Award 1 mark** if all are correct: used as a noun; used as a verb; used as a verb; used as a noun.
Grammar essentials: Some words can be used as both nouns and verbs. Nouns name things and verbs describe actions or states of being.

1

5 **Award 1 mark** if 'sea' is ticked.
Grammar essentials: A root word can be found anywhere in a word and links a word family in spelling and meaning.

1

6 **Award 1 mark** if 'had listened' is underlined.
Grammar essentials: The past perfect tense describes an action that occurred before another action in the past.

1

7 **Award 1 mark** for: A few years from now, self-driving vehicles will be a common sight. (The comma must be included.)
Grammar /punctuation essentials: When an adverbial phrase is placed at the start of a sentence (fronted adverbial), it should be separated from the main clause by a comma.

1

8 **Award 1 mark** for: A flash of lightning lit up the garden; a second later, thunder rattled the windows in their frames.
Grammar essentials: A semi-colon is used to link two main clauses of equal importance about the same subject (here, a storm).

1

9 **Award 1 mark** if all are correct: informal, formal, formal, informal.
Grammar essentials: Formal vocabulary is suitable for official or serious communication; informal vocabulary is more common in everyday speech and writing, including slang and dialect words.

1

10	**Award 1 mark** if all are correct: adopted, swam, slept. **Grammar essentials:** The 'ed' suffix is added to many verbs to form the simple past tense. Irregular verbs don't follow this rule.	1
11	**a. Award 1 mark** if both are correct: month's, wheel's. **b. Award 1 mark** for explanations along the lines of: These words are plural nouns that do not possess anything. **Grammar essentials:** Apostrophes should only be used to show contraction (they are = they're) or to show where something belongs to someone or something (possession). Plural nouns on their own do not need an apostrophe.	2
	Total	12

Q	Mark scheme for Grammar and Punctuation Test 5	Marks
1	**Award 1 mark** if 'until' and 'when' are underlined. **Grammar essentials:** Conjunctions can link words, phrases or clauses.	1
2	**Award 1 mark** if all three are ticked: You promised to help me, didn't you How was the movie Should I go and fill the car up **Grammar essentials:** There are three ways of forming a question: using a question tag (for example, didn't you?); using a question word (for example, how?); or using an inversion (for example, should I?).	1
3	**Award 1 mark** for: Unless the taxi arrives soon, we are going to miss our flight to Paris. (The comma must be included.) **Grammar essentials:** A subordinate clause is introduced by a subordinating conjunction (here 'unless'). When you place a subordinate clause at the start of a sentence, it must be separated by a comma from the main clause that follows it.	1
4	**Award 1 mark** if all are ticked: drowsy, slow, weary. **Grammar essentials:** Synonyms are words with the same meaning. Antonyms are words with the opposite meaning.	1
5	**Award 1 mark** if all are correct: chefs; knives; boxes. **Grammar essentials:** Plural nouns often take the suffix 's' but some have irregular endings.	1
6	Award 1 mark for: There was a figure in the shadows – or was it just my imagination? **Punctuation essentials:** A single dash is used to indicate an interruption or a change of tone or direction.	1
7	**Award 1 mark** for: At summer camp, you can choose from: • learning life-saving skills in the pool • building a shelter in the woods • climbing down the cliffs by the sea **Grammar essentials:** Consistency is the key here. For example, you can accept consistent capitalisation of all three verbs and consistent use of semi-colons at the end of the first two items with a full stop after the third. The conjunction 'or' should not be included.	1
8	**Award 1 mark** if both are correct: are deciding, is running. **Grammar essentials:** The present progressive tense describes events that are still happening in the present.	1
9	**Award 1 mark** for: a prepositional phrase. **Grammar essentials:** A prepositional phrase begins with a preposition (here 'beneath') and ends with a noun, noun phrase or pronoun (here 'the sea').	1
10	**Award 1 mark** for: The concert was delayed by ten minutes again (the violinist was always late). **Punctuation essentials:** Extra information can be included in a sentence using parentheses, which is placed between a pair of commas, brackets or dashes. In this example brackets or a single dash could be used.	1
11	**a. Award 1 mark** if both are ticked: It is all written in the future tense. It contains two adverbs. **b. Award 1 mark** if all are correct: special, beautiful, amazing, tropical. **Grammar essentials:** The present form can be used to express the future tense (here 'the plane leaves at six in the morning'). Adjectives describe nouns and can come before or after the noun.	2
	Total	12

Q	Mark scheme for Grammar and Punctuation Test 6	Marks
1	**Award 1 mark** if the correct sentence is ticked: Diwali is a special time of year for Hindus. It is a festival of lights. **Grammar essentials:** Proper nouns (Diwali, Hindus) need capital letters; common nouns (festival, lights) and adjectives (special) do not.	1
2	**Award 1 mark** for: You were always interested in animals. **Grammar essentials:** A statement states a fact or opinion and uses a full stop.	1
3	**Award 1 mark** if all are correct: necessary. possible. necessary. possible. **Grammar essentials:** Modal verbs are found in front of other verbs. They express degrees of possibility, certainty or necessity.	1
4	**Award 1 mark** for any appropriate replacement for 'criminal'. For example: The **mouse** was caught in a trap. **Grammar essentials:** In the passive sentence, the subject (criminal) is having the action done to it. In a passive as well as an active sentence, the subject comes before the verb.	1
5	**Award 1 mark** if all are correct: sightless, coves, presentation. **Grammar essentials:** A root word can be found anywhere in a word and links a word family in spelling and meaning.	1
6	**Award 1 mark** for: When Molly went swimming, her brother Ashton taught her how to dive. **Grammar essentials:** The past tense is used to describe events that were completed in the past.	1
7	**Award 1 mark** for a correct explanation along the lines of: 'Her sister's friends' refers to one sister; 'her sisters' friends' refers to two or more sisters. **Punctuation essentials:** Apostrophes can be used to show possession. With singular nouns (here 'sister'), you add an apostrophe and then 's'. For plural nouns ending in 's' (here 'sisters'), the apostrophe goes after the 's'.	1
8	**Award 1 mark** if all are correct: Standard English, non-Standard English, Standard English, non-Standard English. **Grammar essentials:** 'Alex and I' is correct as the subject of the sentence, before the verb; 'Alex and me' is correct as the object of the sentence, after the verb.	1
9	**Award 1 mark** if 'a noun phrase' is ticked. **Grammar essentials:** A noun phrase is a group of words that gives more detail about the noun.	1
10	**Award 1 mark** for: "Watch out!" shouted Mum. "The oven is very hot." (Single inverted commas are also acceptable.) **Punctuation essentials:** Inverted commas are also called speech marks. They mark the start and end of the exact words being spoken. Any punctuation associated with the speech also goes inside them.	1
11	**a. Award 1 mark** if 'their' is ticked. **b. Award 1 mark** if 'an adverb' is ticked. **Grammar essentials:** Pronouns replace nouns or noun phrases. Some pronouns show possession ('their' way). Adverbs usually describe verbs, but they are also used to modify adjectives ('very' demanding), as well as other adverbs and clauses.	2
	Total	12

Q	Mark scheme for Grammar and Punctuation Test 7	Marks
1	**Award 1 mark** if the correct sentence is ticked: When you hear the starting pistol, run as fast as you can. **Grammar essentials:** A command gives an order or instruction. It contains an imperative verb (here, 'run').	1
2	**Award 1 mark** for: Fish and chips, pizzas, sausages and kebabs often contain large amounts of fat. **Punctuation essentials:** Commas are used to separate items in a list. Do not put a comma before the final item in well-known noun phrases (here, 'fish and chips').	1
3	**Award 1 mark** if both are correct: As soon as, provided. **Grammar essentials:** Subordinating conjunctions introduce subordinate clauses. Such a clause does not make sense on its own as a sentence.	1
4	**Award 1 mark** for: The two brothers had left school, (had) started a business and (had) become very successful. (Also accept the sentence in the simple past tense: The two brothers left school, started a business and became very successful.) **Grammar essentials:** If the answer is in the past perfect form (had + past tense), the repetition of the word 'had' is optional.	1
5	**Award 1 mark** if both are correct: which were covered in mud; after football in the rain. **Grammar essentials:** The subordinate clause contains a verb (here, 'were'); the adverbial does not. Neither makes sense on its own.	1

6	**Award I mark** if all are correct: could've, it's, shan't. **Grammar /punctuation essentials:** The apostrophe is used to indicate exactly where letters have been removed as two words are contracted. Some contractions are irregular (here, 'shan't' not 'shalln't').	I
7	**Award I mark** if all are correct: Why is **that** person staring? Is that **an** invitation? When are **most** visitors expected? **Grammar essentials:** A determiner is used at the start of a noun phrase to make it more specific or to show quantity or possession.	I
8	**Award I mark** if both are correct: The weary traveller walked along the cliff path. After school, Lenny went to boxing. **Grammar essentials:** Prepositions are used before nouns to indicate place, direction or time. They are not used before clauses.	I
9	**Award I mark** for: The powerful storm destroyed the fishing boats. **Grammar essentials:** In an active sentence, the subject is the thing doing the action to the object.	I
10	**Award I mark** for an explanation along the lines of: The first sentence means that all the passengers were hot and bored. The second sentence means that it was only the passengers that were hot and bored who complained (i.e. there were other passengers who were not hot and bored). **Punctuation essentials:** Commas are used to make meaning clearer. Here, the commas in the first sentence are used to mark the start and end of a relative clause.	I
11	**a. Award I mark** if all are correct: adventurous, artistic, fortunate. **b. Award I mark** for one of the following: unadventurous, unartistic, unfortunate. **Grammar essentials:** Nouns can be made into adjectives by adding a variety of suffixes. Prefixes often make the root word opposite or negative in meaning.	2
	Total	**12**

Q	Mark scheme for Grammar and Punctuation Test 8	Marks
1	**Award I mark** if both are correct: was, lived. **Grammar essentials:** Verbs describe actions (lived) and states of being (was).	I
2	**Award I mark** if 'How irritating that salesman was' is ticked. **Grammar /punctuation essentials:** This exclamation expresses a strong feeling. The word order means that it is not a question like the other examples.	I
3	**Award I mark** if all are correct: These are the places I would like to go one day: Paris in the spring sunshine; the snow-capped mountains of Switzerland; and Cairo with its amazing pyramids. **Punctuation essentials:** Semi-colons can be used to separate expanded noun phrases in a list introduced by a colon.	I
4	**Award I mark** if 'They may come for tea this evening' is ticked. **Grammar essentials:** The words 'may', 'must', 'will' and 'shall' are all modal verbs that show different levels of possibility, certainty or necessity.	I
5	**Award I mark** for: We were really disappointed: the food was cold, the table was dirty and the waiter was rude. **Punctuation essentials:** A colon is used between two main clauses where the second clause gives an explanation of the first.	I
6	**Award I mark** if 'a tiny man from Dundee with an explosion of grey curly hair' is circled. **Grammar essentials:** A relative clause introduces more information about a noun (here, 'the piano tuner'). Note the relative pronoun and verb ('who was') are not used here.	I
7	**Award I mark** if all are correct: pollenate, apologise, classify, televise. **Grammar essentials:** Suffixes can be used to change the word class of a root word.	I
8	**Award I mark** for: He was wearing those shoes that he bought last week. **Grammar essentials:** Standard English is English that uses standard grammatical forms. Here, this means: the subject and verb must agree ('he was' not 'he were'); the correct determiner must be used ('those' not 'them'); and the correct relative pronoun must be used ('that' not 'what').	I

Q		Marks
9	**Award I mark** if all are correct: We told them about the power cut but they went to his house anyway. My rabbit, which loves carrots, likes sleeping on our sofa. **Grammar essentials:** Pronouns replace nouns. Possessive pronouns show who or what something belongs to. Relative pronouns introduce relative clauses and refer back to a noun.	I
10	**Award I mark** for: There was a **hand-made** yellow skirt in the window display. **Grammar /punctuation essentials:** 'Hand-made' is a compound adjective.	I
11	**a. Award I mark** if all are correct: The boys were playing catch in the garden. – past progressive The boys have played catch in the garden. – present perfect The boys played catch in the garden. – simple past The boys had played catch in the garden. – past perfect **b. Award I mark** for: The boys are playing catch in the garden. **Grammar essentials:** There are a number of ways of describing actions in the past tense depending on when they took place and for how long. Progressive means that an action is or was in progress.	I

Total   **12**

Mark scheme for Grammar and Punctuation Test 9

Q		Marks
1	**Award I mark** if all are correct: and, or, but. **Grammar essentials:** Co-ordinating conjunctions join words or clauses of equal importance.	I
2	**Award I mark** if all are correct: boy, school (nouns); pizza (subject). **Grammar essentials:** The subject is the thing doing the action. It comes before the verb in both active and passive sentences; in passive sentences, the subject is a 'passive subject'.	I
3	**Award I mark** if all are correct. Examples include: mistake/retake/overtake; retired/attired/overtired; triangular/rectangular/quadrangular. **Grammar essentials:** A prefix is a group of letters attached to the beginning of a word. It give a word a new meaning. Some prefixes, such as 'un', give a word the opposite meaning but here children are being asked to think of prefixes that give different meanings.	I
4	**Award I mark** for: Last Sunday evening, we watched an amazing nature documentary, whilst my nan fell asleep on the sofa and snored loudly. **Grammar /punctuation essentials:** The first comma separates the fronted adverbial from the main clause. The second comma separates the main clause from the subordinate clause.	I
5	**Award I mark** if all are correct: The girls forgot to buy the chocolates, didn't they? Remember to do your homework, won't you? I guess I should try harder, shouldn't I? After school, we're going swimming, aren't we? **Grammar essentials:** Question tags are one way of forming questions and must match the subject of the sentence.	I
6	**Award I mark** if 'were' is ticked. **Grammar essentials:** The subjunctive is a verb form used to express something that should happen.	I
7	**Award I mark** for: Gethin often goes walking in the mountains but he usually forgets his coat. **Grammar essentials:** The simple present expresses actions that happen regularly or are generally true	I
8	**Award I mark** for: Fatima asked Zara, "Do you want/Would you like to come to a party this evening?" (Single inverted commas are also acceptable.) **Punctuation essentials:** Inverted commas are also called speech marks. They mark the start and end of the exact words being spoken. Any punctuation associated with the speech also goes inside them.	I
9	**Award I mark** if all are correct. Examples include: doubting/doubtless/undoubtable; purity/purify/purely/purest; daily/today/yesterday. **Grammar essentials:** Prefixes and suffixes are added to root words to form other word classes and change meaning.	I
10	**Award I mark** if all are correct: how, when, where. **Grammar essentials:** Adverbs are used to describe when, where and how an action is taking place.	I

11	**a. Award 1 mark** if all are correct: my uncle Joseph, this coming winter (noun phrases); this coming winter is going to be very cold (clause). **b. Award 1 mark** for: verb. **Grammar essentials:** Noun phrases form the subjects and objects in sentences. A clause has to contain at least a subject and a verb.	2
	Total	**12**

Q	Mark scheme for Grammar and Punctuation Test 10	Marks
1	**Award 1 mark** for: My mum is always worrying about losing her purse. I look after my pocket money in a jar, which I keep next to my bed so that no-one can steal it. How do you look after your money? **Grammar /punctuation essentials:** A full stop is at the end of a statement-type sentence. A sentence contains a main clause and may include a number of other linked clauses.	1
2	**Award 1 mark** if both are correct: because, after. We should get off the beach because the tide is about to turn. I must tidy up the house after our visitors have left. **Grammar essentials:** Conjunctions are used to join words, phrases or clauses.	1
3	**Award 1 mark** if both are correct: who was born in Sheffield; while he was eating an ice-cream. **Grammar essentials:** The first subordinate clause is a relative clause. The second subordinate clause is introduced by the conjunction 'while'. Neither subordinate clause makes sense on its own. 'Last week' is not a clause as it does not contain a verb.	1
4	**Award 1 mark** for: had. **Grammar essentials:** The past perfect tense is used to describe an event that occurs before another event in the past.	1
5	**Award 1 mark** if all are correct: conjunction, clause, phrase. **Grammar essentials:** A clause must contain a verb. A conjunction is a linking word /phrase between words, phrases or clauses. A phrase is a group of words that does not contain a subject/verb pair.	1
6	**Award 1 mark** if all are correct: What a fool I've been! – exclamation What did you do? – question I left my passport at home. – statement Go and fetch it quickly! – command **Punctuation essentials:** Exclamations, statements and commands can all end in exclamation marks.	1
7	**Award 1 mark** if all are correct: before, due to, behind. **Grammar essentials:** Prepositions come before nouns or noun phrases to show position, direction or time.	1
8	**Award 1 mark** if all are correct. Singular nouns: dog's, Angus's bag; plural nouns: children's, neighbours'. **Grammar essentials:** 'Children' is a plural noun as it refers to more than one child. However, it is irregular and acts like a singular noun, taking an apostophe followed by 's' to show possession	1
9	**Award 1 mark** if all are correct: importance, instance, resistance, appearance. **Grammar essentials:** Root words can be changed into different word classes by adding suffixes.	1
10	**Award 1 mark** for any suitable additional information that refers back to the bird by using a relative pronoun. For example: The strange bird, **which only ate snails**, flapped its wings and flew away. **Grammar essentials:** Relative clauses often start with a relative pronoun: 'who', 'whose', 'which' or 'that'.	1
11	**Award 1 mark** if all are correct: The tall wizard, who lived in a tower full of cobwebs, cast a spell on the village. His parcel finally arrived (it was already two months late). When he found his spelling mistakes – there were over 100 of them – the author shook his head in horror. **b. Award 1 mark** if 'a parenthesis' is ticked. **Punctuation essentials:** A pair of commas, dashes or brackets can be used to add a parenthesis (additional information) to a sentence.	2
	Total	**12**

How to administer the spelling tests

There are ten short spelling tests in this book. Each test consists of four questions and should take approximately ten minutes to complete, although you should allow your child as much time as they need to complete them.

Read the instructions in the box below. The instructions are similar to the ones given in the National Curriculum tests. This will familiarise children with the style and format of the tests and show them what to expect.

> *Listen carefully to the instructions I am going to give you.*
>
> *I am going to read four sentences to you. Each sentence on your answer sheet has a missing word. Listen carefully to the missing word and write it in the space provided, making sure you spell the word correctly.*
>
> *I will read the word, then the word within the sentence, then repeat the word a third time.*
>
> *Do you have any questions?*

Read the spellings as follows:

- Give the question number, 'Spelling 1'
- Say, 'The word is...'
- Read the whole sentence to show the word in context.
- Repeat, 'The word is...'

Leave at least a 12-second gap between each spelling.

At the end re-read all four questions. Then say, 'This is the end of the test. Please put down your pencil or pen.'

Each correct answer should be awarded **1 mark**.

Spelling test transcripts

Spelling test 1

Spelling 1: The word is **friend**.
Ollie was Joshua's new best **friend**.
The word is **friend**.

Spelling 2: The word is **thought**.
Evie **thought** it was probably time to
go home.
The word is **thought**.

Spelling 3: The word is **dictionary**.
You can use a **dictionary** to look up word
meanings.
The word is **dictionary**.

Spelling 4: The word is **chemistry**.
Riley enjoyed **chemistry** and biology
at school.
The word is **chemistry**.

Spelling test 2

Spelling 1: The word is **machine**.
The washing **machine** was making a
strange noise.
The word is **machine**.

Spelling 2: The word is **temperature**.
The **temperature** soared in the desert.
The word is **temperature**.

Spelling 3: The word is **preferred**.
My Uncle Stan always **preferred** to drink
cold tea.
The word is **preferred**.

Spelling 4: The word is **bicycle**.
Rohan took his broken **bicycle** to the
recycling centre.
The word is **bicycle**.

Spelling test 3

Spelling 1: The word is **ceiling**.
Water from the bath was dripping
through the **ceiling**.
The word is **ceiling**.

Spelling 2: The word is **plague**.
The town was invaded by a **plague** of rats.
The word is **plague**.

Spelling 3: The word is **guessed**.
Denise **guessed** most of the answers
in the test.
The word is **guessed**.

Spelling 4: The word is **treasure**.
The pirate captain dropped the **treasure** map
overboard.
The word is **treasure**.

Spelling test 4

Spelling 1: The word is **flyweight**.
The boxer entered the **flyweight** competition.
The word is **flyweight**.

Spelling 2: The word is **submerged**.
The shipwreck was **submerged** beneath
the waves.
The word is **submerged**.

Spelling 3: The word is **scientist**.
Flora decided she wanted to become
a **scientist**.
The word is **scientist**.

Spelling 4: The word is **sensation**.
Spicy food can cause a burning **sensation** in
your mouth.
The word is **sensation**.

Spelling test transcripts

Spelling test 5

Spelling 1: The word is **ferocious**.
The great lion let out a **ferocious** roar.
The word is **ferocious**.

Spelling 2: The word is **social**.
Children should be careful when using **social** networks.
The word is **social**.

Spelling 3: The word is **marvellous**.
The school fair was a **marvellous** success.
The word is **marvellous**.

Spelling 4: The word is **available**.
My favourite sweets are no longer **available** in the shops.
The word is **available**.

Spelling test 6

Spelling 1: The word is **vacancy**.
My mum is looking for a job **vacancy** near home.
The word is **vacancy**.

Spelling 2: The word is **magician**.
The **magician** practised his tricks for hour after hour.
The word is **magician**.

Spelling 3: The word is **cautiously**.
A tiny mouse crept out **cautiously** from behind the fridge.
The word is **cautiously**.

Spelling 4: The word is **environmental**.
Samit was very interested in **environmental** matters.
The word is **environmental**.

Spelling test 7

Spelling 1: The word is **scene**.
Mia used watercolours to paint the beautiful **scene**.
The word is **scene**.

Spelling 2: The word is **frantically**.
The swimmer was **frantically** waving for help.
The word is **frantically**.

Spelling 3: The word is **invasion**.
General Fox ordered the **invasion** to begin the next day.
The word is **invasion**.

Spelling 4: The word is **passed**.
The sports car accelerated and **passed** the slow lorry.
The word is **passed**.

Spelling test 8

Spelling 1: The word is **protein**.
The human body uses **protein** to build and repair muscles.
The word is **protein**.

Spelling 2: The word is **immediately**.
You should wash a burn **immediately** under cold running water.
The word is **immediately**.

Spelling 3: The word is **professional**.
Tijan dreamed about becoming a **professional** footballer.
The word is **professional**.

Spelling 4: The word is **enough**.
We didn't have **enough** petrol for the journey.
The word is **enough**.

Spelling test transcripts

Spelling test 9

Spelling 1: The word is **misleading**.
The instructions for building the furniture were **misleading**.
The word is **misleading**.

Spelling 2: The word is **through**.
The bullet travelled straight **through** the brick.
The word is **through**.

Spelling 3: The word is **beginners**.
Otto was put in the group for **beginners**.
The word is **beginners**.

Spelling 4: The word is **incredibly**.
Incredibly, the injured climber managed to survive.
The word is **incredibly**.

Spelling test 10

Spelling 1: The word is **technique**.
The sprinter was always trying to improve his **technique**.
The word is **technique**.

Spelling 2: The word is **interference**.
Storms can cause **interference** with TV and radio broadcasts.
The word is **interference**.

Spelling 3: The word is **accept**.
Luke couldn't **accept** that he had lost the game.
The word is **accept**.

Spelling 4: The word is **explanation**.
My grandma left suddenly without **explanation**.
The word is **explanation**.

Progress chart

Fill in your score in the table below to see how well you've done.

Test number (Grammar, Punctuation and Spelling)	Score
Test 1	
Test 2	
Test 3	
Test 4	
Test 5	
Test 6	
Test 7	
Test 8	
Test 9	
Test 10	
TOTAL	

Mark	
0–50	Good try! You need more practice in some topics – ask an adult to help you.
51–110	You're doing really well. Ask for extra help for any topics you found tricky.
111–160	You're a 10-Minute SATs Test grammar, punctuation and spelling star – good work!

GREAT WORK!

Reward Certificate

Well done!

You have completed all of the 10-Minute SATs Tests

Name: _____   Date: _____

QUICK TESTS FOR SATs SUCCESS

BOOST YOUR CHILD'S CONFIDENCE WITH 10-MINUTE SATs TESTS

-  Bite-size mini SATs tests which take just 10 minutes to complete
- Covers key National Test topics
- Full answers and progress chart provided to track improvement
- Available for Years 2 and 6

Find out more at www.scholastic.co.uk